The Dressing-up Book

Jane Bull

DK

Dorling Kindersley

LONDON, NEW YORK, MUNICH,
MELBOURNE, AND DELHI

DESIGN • Jane Bull
EDITOR • Penelope Arlon
PHOTOGRAPHY • Andy Crawford
DESIGN ASSISTANT • Gemma Fletcher

PUBLISHING MANAGER • Sue Leonard
PRODUCTION • Angela Graef
DTP DESIGNER • Almudena Díaz

For Charlotte, Billy, and James

First published in Great Britain in 2006 by
Dorling Kindersley Limited
80 Strand, London WC2R 0RL

A Penguin Company

2 4 6 8 10 9 7 5 3 1

A CIP catalogue record for this book
is available from the British Library

ISBN 13: 978-1-4053-1307-0

ISBN 10: 1-4053-1307-2

Colour reproduction by
GRB Editrice S.r.l., Verona, Italy
Printed and bound by Toppan, China

discover more at
www.dk.com

I'm off to find that treasure!

A book full of characters...

become a rubbish robot...

...or star on TV!

Let's dress up!

what's in the dressing-up box?

Mum's shoes, Dad's shirt,

Granny's handbag,

Auntie's beads?

Beads

Boots and shoes

Clothes

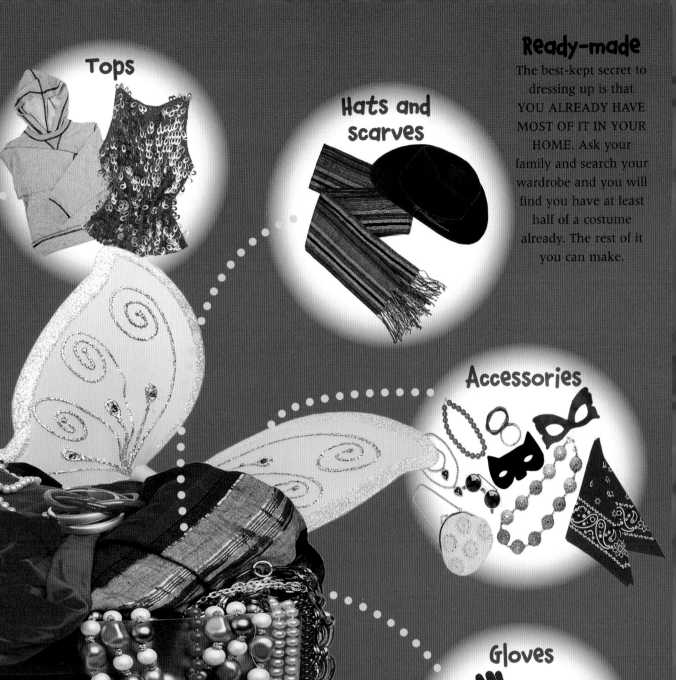

Tops

Hats and scarves

Accessories

Gloves

The best-kept secret to dressing up is that YOU ALREADY HAVE MOST OF IT IN YOUR HOME. Ask your family and search your wardrobe and you will find you have at least half of a costume already. The rest of it you can make.

DIY costume

Using a little imagination and spending a little time on a costume is not only satisfying but guarantees an original costume every time. You don't want to hire one and find someone else has had the same idea!

Beads and boas

Look out Mum! We're after your frills and fancies, for our own fashion parade.

Bags of beads

On the catwalk

Most mums have a secret stash of beads and bangles that they haven't used for years. Get your friends to ask their mums too and hold a fashion show.

Little angel

This little angel has home-made wings. Find out how to make them yourself on page 44.

Cool sunglasses

And the winner is...

Your catwalk wouldn't be complete without music and a microphone – make your own on page 48.

Feathers

For instant glamour, who can resist floaty, feathery boas.

Mum's dress

Wear it over your t-shirt.

Mum's top

It doubles as a dress!

Pile on the beads, swish about with a boa, and teeter along in high heels.

Use a red towel as a cape.

DIY heroes

An alien, a pirate, a witch, or Super-Boy – raid your own wardrobe and you'll be surprised what you can create with a little imagination.

What makes a pirate? A stripy t-shirt and rolled-up trousers.

Witch

What makes a witch? Stripy tights!

Imp

See how to make my wings on page 44

Turn to page 42 to find out how to make a witch's cape.

Skipping-rope lasso

Alien

Paint a face onto a balloon and pop it inside a hooded top. A very tall alien – it's out of this world!

Yellow rubber gloves

Yee ha! cowboy

A check shirt, a skipping-rope lasso, and a neckerchief are the basics for a cracking cowboy costume.

Super-Boy

Black tights, red socks, and a red towel as a cape. Save the world Super-Boy!

Safety pin the cape to your t-shirt.

Mini pirate

He's found the treasure!

You will need:

A mop, three pieces of cane, sticky tape, string, a stapler, a large shirt, and bits and bobs to make the body.

Tape a small cane to the top of the mop for the shoulders.

Ask your Dad for an old shirt.

The hand canes need to be the same length as the mop.

Gentle giant

Hello down there! Walk tall with the amazing smiling, waving giant. Find yourself a mop, a huge shirt, and two good friends to help him wave.

Decorate the face using a toilet-roll nose and coloured card.

Drape the shirt over the cane shoulders leaving a button undone for the mop holder to see out of.

Giant head

Cut a giant face shape out of thick card and decorate it. Don't worry about the hair – the mop does the trick! Tape the face under the mop.

Make sure the face is positioned so that the mop hair falls in style.

Hello, I'm up here!

Gently move the hand canes from side to side and your giant will wave goodbye.

I'm in here!
Put one of your friends inside the large shirt to hold the mop, and the other two will hold the hands.

Tie a piece of string around the hand and tape the string ends to the cane.

Giant hands
Draw around your hands, but twice the size, on a piece of thick card, and cut out. Tie a piece of string around the cane, then around the hand.

Staple the shirt sleeves to the hand.....

Practise together to give your giant the best moves.

Welcome to Box TV!

I'm Katie Kard, here's the news. A box mania is sweeping the country. Everyone is going box crazy! Our reporter Colin Carton is in the field. What can you tell us Colin?

Box TV

Make a Box TV

To become newsreader Katie Kard, cut a square hole in the side of a box. Glue a strip of kitchen foil around the edge and some bottle lids along the bottom as knobs. Now climb inside and get reporting.

For the aerial, bend a metal coat hanger in half...  ...and tape it to the top of the box.

Yes that's right Katie, it's raining boxes out here! All over the country cardboard boxes are being magically transformed into awesome outfits. Check out these gallant knights and fairy princesses on horseback, yee-ha rodeo cowboys, and recycled robots. Viewers – it's all the rage so get wrapping! And that just about wraps it up for me too.

This is Colin Carton for Box TV back to the studio

Find out how to make the microphone on page 48.

13

The big box cover-up

The first step towards getting boxed up is to find a box as big as you!
When you have found it you need to learn how to wrap it up.

Choose your box

Find the biggest box you can. Decide which is the top, bottom, and sides, and cut the flaps off or tape them down.

Cut out holes for your arms and head.

Ask an adult: to help you cut out the holes and get your box ready.

Cover-up materials

Large pieces of paper, rolls of gift wrap, kitchen foil, and brown packing paper are all perfect for wrapping boxes.

16

How to cover up

1 Lay your box on the rolled-out paper, wrap it around the box, and trim the end.

Turn the box on its side.

Trim the paper so it fits around the corner of the box.

Fold the paper inside the edge of the box and tape it in place.

2 Flatten the paper down the sides of the box.

3 Tape the paper down ignoring the holes at this stage.

4 Cut pieces of paper to cover the sides of the box and tape in position.

Turn the box on its side.

Holes for head and arms

Find the holes and carefully cut slits in the paper. Fold them inside and tape.

Ask an adult: to help cut out the holes.

Tape the paper in position.

Now turn the page to decorate.

All wrapped up!

15

walking gift boxes

Very special delivery – wrap yourself up as an enormous present and deliver yourself to the party!

You will need:
- 1 large wrapped box (see page 15)
- Coloured paper for ribbons and stars
- Sticky tape
- Glue stick

Cut lots of stars out of coloured paper or card.

Add ribbons

Cut some paper strips long enough to fit around your box.

Wrap one around the length of your box and tuck into the neck hole. Tape in place.

Tape another strip around the width of the box.

You could try circle and moon shapes too.

Use glue stick to hold them in place.

Mega box

If you find a really
big box, try making
the hole at the
front for your face
to peep through.

Hello down
there!

If you use rolls
of festive gift
wrap, there is
no need to add
extra decorations.

Make a paper
bow and attach
it to a hairband.

These snazzy socks
match this spotty
box. Find some
of your own and
match your box too.

Recycled robots

" **My name is Box-bot** and if you follow my instructions I can help you recreate me. "

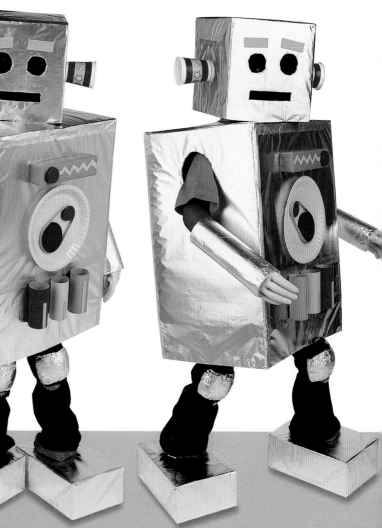

18

Building Box-bot

All you need for this brilliant bot is lots of boxes – big and small – and other cartons, paper plates, and anything else that can be recycled. Silver-painted knee-pads, shoe-box shoes, and a pair of rubber gloves just finish him off.

Ask an adult: to help cut out the holes.

Cut out the robot face.

Head box

Cardboard tubes for arms.

Body box

Stick on drinking cups for ears.

These are the pads you use with your roller blades.

Knee pads

Add some cardboard rolls to look like controls.

Cut a hole to put your foot through.

Shoe box

Wow! Is it a real robot?

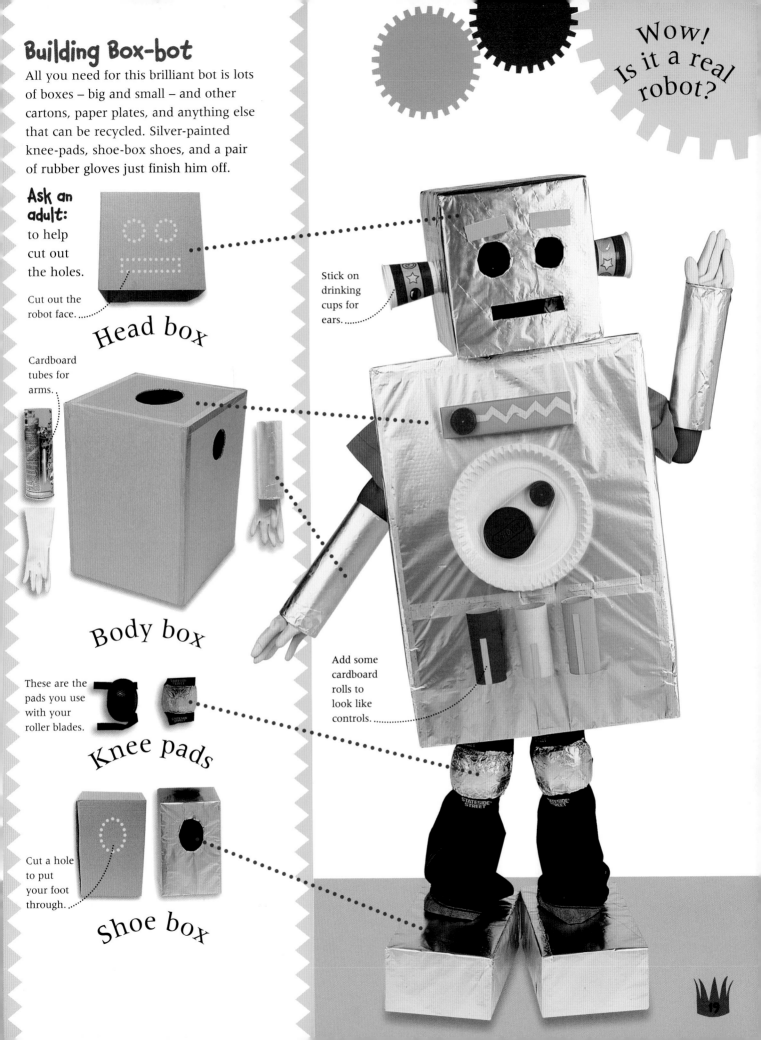

Catch you later fairy friends!

Giddy-up horsey

Get on your horse and galloping into battle or a

yeee haa!

whoa steady boy!

Horsey types

There are so many different horsey themes you could try, such as Black Beauty with a white star on its forehead or a mythical Pegasus with wings.

off you go! Become a knight with your trusty steed cowboy on the prairie, and is there a fairy horse here too?

Horse boxes

Find a large box and turn it on its side. It needs to be big enough for you to fit inside and for your pretend legs to hang over the side.

Start collecting your horsey boxes

21

Make your galloping horses

Follow these steps and you'll end up with a basic horse shape. You can then decorate it how you like or turn the pages for some wild ideas.

Horse body

Find a cardboard box that's big enough for you to fit inside.

Cut off the long flaps at the top and all the bottom flaps. ....

Use strong parcel tape to secure the short flaps. ....

Cut out some coloured paper and stick it to each end first.

Fold the paper over neatly and tape in place.

Measure the paper against the box and cut it to size.

You could snip the bottom edge of the paper into a pattern.

When you have stuck the ends down, glue the sides in place.

Horse head

Draw a simple horse's head shape onto a piece of cardboard.

Cut out the shape then trace both sides onto coloured paper (see bottom).

90° angle

Tape the head in place on the box. ....

To hide the tape, stick strips of paper over it. .

Snip the end of the nose off each piece of coloured paper and glue onto both sides of the head. ..

As a guide, lay the card shape on the coloured paper and draw around it, then turn it over and draw it again. Cut out both shapes.

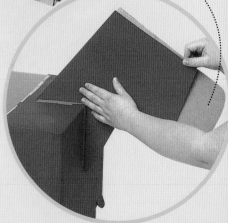

Reins

For sturdy reins to control your wild horse, thread some ribbon through the nose.

To add a noseband, cut a strip of paper and stick it along the nose line.

Ask an adult: to help make the hole.

Use the point of a pen to make a hole big enough to thread some ribbon through for reins.

Tail

Make a tail out of a piece of paper the same colour as the horse.

Cut out a large square piece of paper to the length you want for the tail.

Fold the paper over and over and cut it into strips, leaving the top uncut.

Stick the tail onto the horse with sticky tape.

Shoulder straps

Use ribbon for the straps. Attach them to the box and adjust the length so your horse hangs at the right height.

Make four holes with the point of a pen.

Ask an adult: to help make the holes.

Feed the ribbon through the holes and tie a knot in each end.

Thread ribbon through the holes in the nose for the reins.

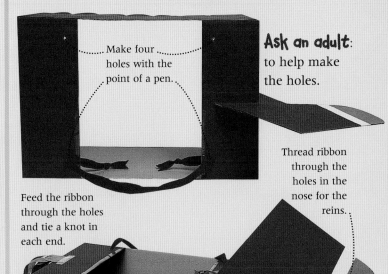

If the straps are too long tie the knot further up to make the strap shorter.

Tip If the straps slip off your shoulders, tape them together at the back.

Now let's show them how to decorate you

Horsey types

How many are there?
About as many as your imagination can stretch to. Magical beasts like a unicorn and a Pegasus can be all sorts of colours, while cowboys might prefer a more natural horse colour.

Fake legs
Take a pair of long socks and stuff them with kitchen foil (this makes them easy to shape). Tape them to the box as shown and glue the foot to the side.

Use strong glue on the socks.

Tape the leg to the inside of the box.

Ears

Cut two ear shapes out of paper, fold them over at the base and glue together. Attach to the head using double-sided tape.

Use the shoulder straps to carry your horse about.

Choose some suitable trousers or tights to wear underneath the horse.

Fake legs made from trousers

Cowboy's legs
Instead of stuffed socks for legs, try draping a pair of trousers across the horse, then stuffing the leg end into some shoes.

26

Magical Unicorn

A unicorn must have a horn. This one is made from card and covered in gold paper and ribbon. Gather together all your sparkly bits and bobs for this special horse.

Gold paper and glitter

Tape the horn onto the head before covering the head with pink paper.

Cut out pink paper flowers and stick them on.

Golden ribbon reins

Pink ribbon mane

Use shiny paper, fabric, and tinsel for decoration.

Knight rider

Regal reds and heraldic shields.

Make an eye with white paper stuck to a yellow oval shape.

Mark on the nose, eye, and mouth with felt pen.

Yellow paper spots help to make a regal cape.

Make a heraldic shield from coloured paper.

Prairie boy

A piebald pony with brown paper patches.

Mark on the nose and mouth with felt pen.

Red paper strips make the bridle straps.

Cut out blobby shapes from brown paper and stick them on with glue.

Cut out a saddle shape from black paper.

25

A knight in shining armour

A true knight needs full armour and weapons. A simple tunic, a shield, a helmet, and a sword are perfect for a shining knight.

Cardboard tube sword
Use the tube from inside a roll of gift wrap. A small tube makes a good dagger.

Take a long tube and squash it flat.

Snip one end into a point.

Cover the whole sword with kitchen foil, then tape a strip of red paper around the handle end.

Wrap some sticky tape around the end.

Cut out a small rectangle of cardboard, paint it black, and cut a slit through the centre.

Slide the cardboard onto the handle end.

The perfect, shining sword.

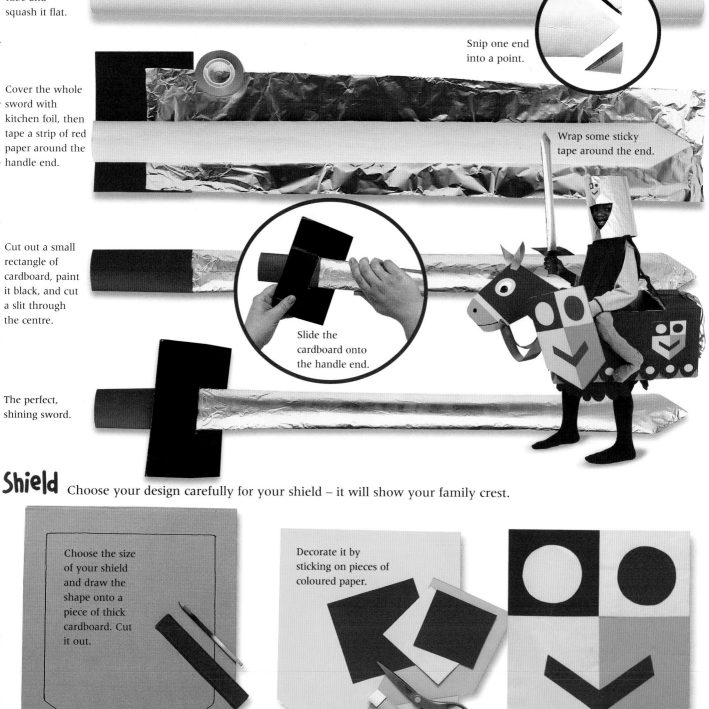

Shield
Choose your design carefully for your shield – it will show your family crest.

Choose the size of your shield and draw the shape onto a piece of thick cardboard. Cut it out.

Decorate it by sticking on pieces of coloured paper.

Make sure the shield has the same pattern as the one on the horse.

Tunic

The idea for this is simple – take a long piece of material, fold it in half, cut a slash along the fold for your head to go through, and tie it around the waist with a belt.

Belt

Cut a slit along the fold – big enough to fit your head through.

Grey woolly gloves

Knight's outfit

To create the right look, wear a hooded top under your tunic – good for the chain-mail effect. Long grey socks and gloves also go well with the outfit. Now pick up your shield, helmet, and sword and become the knight in shining armour.

Make a handle.

Stick a strip of card to the back of a shield as a handle for you to hold it with.

Long grey socks

Helmet

Cut a strip of cardboard long enough to wrap around your head, and taller than the distance from your shoulder to the top of your head.

Draw a triangle in the centre of the strip that will be the face hole.

Cut the face hole out, making sure it is in the right place, and tape the helmet's ends together.

Turn the helmet upside-down and draw around it on cardboard.

Cut the shape out.

Tape the lid onto the helmet, cover it in kitchen foil, and decorate with your crest.

Pirates on the high seas

Ha harr me hearties jump aboard,
we're off to find the treasure!

You could make
a sabre similar to
the knight's sword
on page 26.

Sea legs
Wear blue tights to
look like the sea.

Ship ahoy!
A cardboard box pirate ship,
a Jolly Roger flag, and a
lethal sabre together with a
bag of provisions, and you
are ready to sail the high seas
to find the hidden treasure!

Mmm...
good treasure,
lucky I found it!

Anchors aweigh!
Find a piece of thick cardboard for your ship's anchor.

Draw the shape
Draw an anchor shape and cut it out.

Wrap in foil
Fold the foil around the card, shape it, and tape it down.

Hang it on your boat
Tie some string through the hole and tape it to your boat.

Find me some jewels

Treasure chest
Make a treasure chest to complete your pirate look. Find a box with a lid, decorate it with paper and fill it up with all your jewels and pieces of eight.

Tape a piece of card to a stick for a Jolly Roger flag.

Land ahoy!

How to make your boat

Follow the steps to show you how to make a boat. But remember, it doesn't have to end up as a pirate ship, you could add go-faster white stripes for a speedy power boat.

Boat shape

Try to find a cardboard box that you can fit inside – you also want it to be quite long.

Cut off the long flaps from the top and all the flaps off the bottom.

Use parcel tape to secure the small flaps.

Cut out a piece of card that will curve onto the front of the boat.

Make sure it is taped securely.

Tape it to both sides.

Cut a piece of card to fit on top of the front.

Tape it into place.

Cover the boat

Now you have your basic boat shape, it's time to wrap it. Use coloured paper – brown parcel paper is a good option.

When you reach the curved front, attach a sheet that is slightly taller than the boat.

Snip the overhang down to the top of the boat all along as shown.

Lay each bit flat and tape in place.

Finally cut a piece of paper to fit on the top at the front and stick in place – this will hide the messy bits.

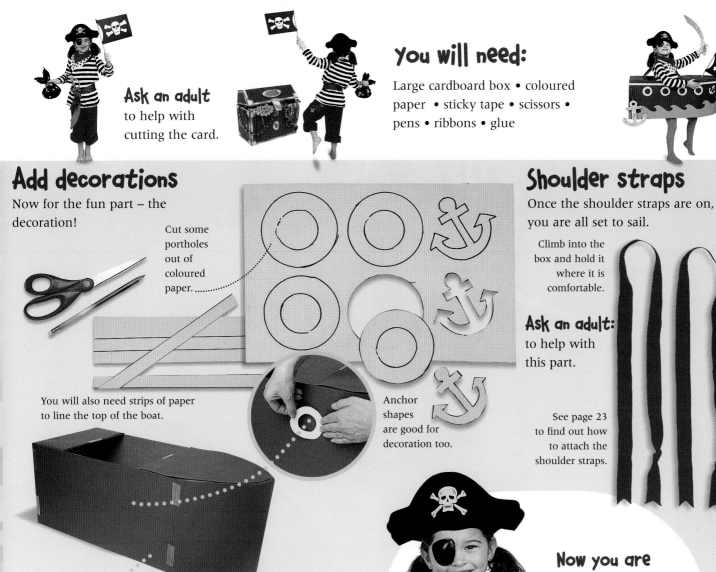

Ask an adult to help with cutting the card.

You will need:

Large cardboard box • coloured paper • sticky tape • scissors • pens • ribbons • glue

Add decorations

Now for the fun part – the decoration!

Cut some portholes out of coloured paper.

You will also need strips of paper to line the top of the boat.

Anchor shapes are good for decoration too.

Stick a band of waves onto the bottom of your boat.

Draw a wave shape on blue paper and cut it out.

Shoulder straps

Once the shoulder straps are on, you are all set to sail.

Climb into the box and hold it where it is comfortable.

Ask an adult: to help with this part.

See page 23 to find out how to attach the shoulder straps.

Now you are ready for the high seas!

Car body

You will need a cardboard box, large enough for you to fit inside.

Cut all the flaps off the bottom of the box.

Cut the long flaps off the top.

Tape the short ends down.

Wrap the box up with coloured paper.

See page 22 for wrapping tips.

Car parts

Collect together some bits and bobs for decoration.

Paper cup

Paper bowls or plates

Cardboard tubes and boxes

Driving in my car

Attach some straps – follow the steps on page 23.

Paper-plate steering wheel.

Paint black lines for the doors.

I like driving in my cardboard car. It gets me here, there, and everywhere!

beep beep!

32

Car parts

You will need paper plates, paper cups, kitchen foil, and some coloured paper to make your car parts.

Headlights and grill

Paper bowl

Wrap two paper bowls in foil.

Stick two paper circles inside.

Wrap a box in foil and add black stripes for the grill. Stick them on with double-sided tape.

Bumpers

Silver foil

Cardboard tube from inside the foil.

Wrap two tubes and tuck in the ends.

Rear lights

Paper cup

Glue some red coloured paper inside them.

Cut two cups in half.

Wrap them in foil.

Use double-sided sticky tape to attach the decorations to the car.

Wheels

Paper bowl or plate

Glue two circles of paper to the plate.

Paint on the tyres.

... A box wrapped in yellow paper makes a good boot.

Along the roads . . .

beep beep!

around the bends . . .

I then . . .

. . . stop off to see my friends.

Fairy princess

with a swish of the wand

become a princess from tip to toe.

A fairy outfit

To create the fairy look you need a paper crown, a pink t-shirt tucked into a paper skirt, and fancy slippers. Finish it off with bangles and beads AND of course, a floaty cape (see page 43).

Crown

Lots and lots of pink beads.

A t-shirt, leotard, or even a swimming costume, just as long as it's pink!

T-shirt

Crepe-paper skirt

Skirt

Tie a gold bow to your shoes to add some fairy sparkle.

Shoes

A magic wand

Cut out two gold-card stars. Tape one to the end of a long stick then glue the other on top. Decorate the stick with a ribbon.

How to make a fairy float

Crepe paper is great to use – it's tough but flimsy like fabric. You don't just have to make a pink one – try a green and purple one for a Halloween fairy.

Waistband

Cut a piece of gold card about 5 cm (2 in) wide and long enough to fit around your waist with 15 cm (6 in) extra to fasten it.

Fold the paper over and over.

Cut along the fold lines, but not all the way to the top.

Crepe-paper skirt

Cut out sheet of crepe paper wide enough to fit around your waist with an overlap, and long enough to reach your knees.

Draw the shape on the bottom.

Snip around the shape.

Fairy crown

You can't be a proper fairy without a fairy crown! Use your leftover gold card and crepe paper to magic up a crown fit for a fairy princess.

Tape the ends of the card together to make the crown shape.

Cut the strips about 5 cm (2 in) wide and long enough to fit around your head with a bit extra for fastening.

1 Cut a strip of gold card and two pieces of crepe paper.

Cut the card and paper into points.

Tape the crepe paper to the back of the card.

2 Tape the paper strips to the back of the card.

First apply the glue, then sprinkle the glitter.

Glue

Glitter

3 Decorate with glitter and leave to dry before taping the ends together.

Now do the same with another piece of crepe paper – try doing different lengths.

Unfold the paper.

Keep taping on layers of paper.

Tape the paper to the back of the gold card.

With PVA glue, squeeze some shapes on the front of your skirt.

Pink magic

Finish off your fairy outfit by adding pink accessories. Search around your house – you may find some pink beads and bangles to wear. Turn to page 43 to find out how to make the fairy cape.

Fasten your skirt with Velcro.

Sprinkle glitter on the glue and let it dry.

The spooks are out

when the moon is full

watch out for the ghosts and ghouls, bats flying by, and visits from strange aliens.

Look out! Those bones are dancing!

Take me to your leader

38

Take cover!
There's a
ghost in
the house.

Screaming spooks

Send shivers down spines at witching hour by becoming this spooky spectre.

Ask your mum if she has a spare white sheet.

Draw some spooky eyes and a mouth shape out of black felt and cut them out.

Creepy costume

The spooky ghost is a great costume for a Halloween party but you may have to take it off when you want to eat or chat, so make sure you wear party clothes underneath it.

Stick the eyes and mouth onto the sheet with PVA glue and cut tiny holes in the eyes for you to see out of.

Try the sheet out for size. You may have to trim it – you don't want to trip up.

Skull mask

A good skeleton needs a skull mask.

Take a paper plate and draw these outlines on it.

Cut along these lines.

Overlap the flap where you have made the slits at the top.

Glue in place on both sides.

Draw holes where your eyes will go and cut them out.

Cut eyes, a nose and teeth out of black card.

Make a hole on each side of the face and thread some elastic through to tie it around your head.

Knot

Stick the features on with glue.

Wear your mask with your funny bones outfit.

Funny bones

No one will be laughing at these funny bones –
they'll be shaking in their shoes!

Find yourself a black pair of trousers and a black top – a turtle neck works well.

Measure how big your bones will be on your clothes.

Put double-sided tape on the reverse.

Draw out the bones on white card.

Cut the bones out.

Learn how to make a bat outfit on page 42.

Mr Bones

Pop on your mask and your funny-bones outfit and go out dancing! To get the best out of your costume, stand in front of a dark, preferably black, background.

Bat cape

Glove

Glove

Create your cape

You need a piece of black fabric for your cape. To measure how much, hold the fabric with outstretched arms and that will be your widest edge. Fold it in half to cut it.

Attach the gloves to the material with a safety pin.

You will need:

Black fabric
Gloves
Hat and mask
Safety pins
Pen or chalk for marking fabric
Scissors/pinking shears

Cut the fabric

Take a square piece of fabric and fold it in half.

Draw the cape pattern with chalk, making sure the fold is on the left side.

Cut the fabric with pinking shears or carefully with scissors.

All you need for your bat outfit is a black top, black leggings, and black shoes.

Bat hat

Mask

Cut a mask shape out of card, poke a hole in each side, and thread a piece of string through them.

Bat ears

It's just a woolly hat with some paper ears.

Cut two ear shapes out of black paper.

Pin the ears to the hat with a safety pin.

Pin the centre of the cape to your top with a safety pin.

Fairy cape

Create your cape

As with the bat cape, find a large piece of pink material and hold it out with your arms outstretched. This will be the width of your cape. Cut it into a large rectangle and fold the material in half.

Tie each end of the cape onto a bracelet.

Cut it out

Fold the fabric in half and draw on the pattern as shown, making sure the fold is on the left side.

Cut the fabric out with scissors or pinking shears.

Use safety pins to attach the cape to your t-shirt.

43

wings for things

Everyone needs wings at some point in their life. And they are so simple to make.

Angel

Impish bat

wing shape

Choose the shape that you would like your wings to be – soft lines for the fairy or angel wings, or pointed for the impish ones. You will need thick cardboard to make the wings – try a large cardboard box.

Fold a piece of paper in half and draw the shape of your wing on it.

......Fold

Unfold the paper and lay it on a big piece of thick cardboard. Draw around it.

Ask an adult: to help you cut out the wing shape.

Lay the shape on coloured paper, draw around it and cut it out.

Glue the paper onto the wings.

Glitter and sparkle

Now for the fun bit! It's time to add a bit of a shine to your wings. You could sprinkle some glitter onto them or decorate them with pieces of coloured paper – cut up magazine works well.

Make four holes using the tip of a pen.

Ask an adult: to help you make the holes.

Back view

......Thread two pieces of elastic through the holes as straps.

Front view

......Cut out coloured paper and glue it on.

Use PVA glue (see page 47).......

Add glitter

Glue a pattern on your wings, then sprinkle on the glitter. When you have covered the glue, shake it off onto a sheet of newspaper.

No-sew dressing up

Clever scissors

Pinking shears mean no hemming.

Velcro

Velcro is a great way to attach clothing. Make sure you buy the Velcro with the sticky back.

Pinking shears

Cut the edge of your outfit with these scissors to stop the material from fraying.

Ask an adult

When you read this, always ask an adult to help you.

this book can be made without sewing machines or hand sewing. You may

safety pins and Velcro. Pinking shears are also useful for a "no fray" edge.

Staplers

Costumes are often worn only a few times, so a stapler can be used instead of sewing. They are particularly useful when working with fabric and card together.

Safety pins

Safety pins are the most useful when you are attaching fabric to fabric, for example attaching the fairy cape to a t-shirt.

Buy them in bunches.

Sticky tapes and glues

It is essential that you are equipped with sticky tape and glue when you are making costumes.

Make sure you have them to hand before you start.

Parcel tape

Thick parcel tape is useful when working with cardboard boxes.

Sticky tape

Thin tape is better for smaller accessories.

Double-sided tape

Double-sided tape is a clean way of attaching paper and card together, and it's strong too.

Glue stick is great for sticking paper to paper...

Glue stick

... but PVA is stronger and is better when working with cardboard AND covering with glitter.

PVA glue

Ask an adult: it's always worth asking an adult to help you stick things.

Microphone

A handy prop for reporters, pop stars, and important news. As seen on page 12.

You will need:

A ball
A cardboard tube
Kitchen foil
Black paper
Sticky tape
Cord or string

Tape the ball to the top of the tube.

Wrap the foil around the ball and tape it down.

Wrap some black paper around the tube.

Tape the paper in place.

Tape the end of the cord to the inside of the tube.

Index

Acknowledgements

With thanks to:
Thomas Arlon, James Bull, Jordan Clarkson, Eleanor Coldwell, Evie Coldwell, Renae Dawes, Olivia Hurdle, Daniel Olorunfemi, and Louis Stride for being model heroes.

All images © Dorling Kindersley. For further information see: www.dkimages.com